KATHA UPANISHAD.
De-gendering Hinduism.

SERIES EDITOR: TAPATI BHARADWAJ.

Published by

LIES AND BIG FEET

ISBN: 9384281069
ISBN-13: 978-9384281069

PREFATORY NOTE:

This rendition of an Upanishadic text is but a part of a larger series; the aim of this work is to construe Hindu religious texts as literature, and examine them within a gendered inflected analytical framework. What prevents us from examining the Upanishadic or the Vedic texts within a literary or a gendered perspective? If the basis of religion is "revealed knowledge," which was made evident to men – then is it not obvious that these notions of the Absolute Being would but be defined within gender inflected terminologies? The personal gender-biases of men would affect and predetermine how the notions of the Supreme Being were written about.

Let me explain with an example from an Upanishad. In the <u>Aitareya Upanishad</u>, the first stanza reads in the following manner:

"Om! In the beginning this was but the Absolute Self alone. There was nothing else whatsoever that winked. It thought, 'Let Me create the world.'"

We have to keep in mind that the Vedic texts are partially truthful – they are correct in their explanations on the notion of Absolute Consciousness which becomes matter, and there is no gender ascribed to this Absolute Being. The "Absolute Self" is denoted within gender neutral terms and is referred to as "It."

But there is a slippage which occurs in the Vedic texts, making these texts suspect: it reveals the fact that those who were writing about this kind of revealed, divine knowledge were men and their interests are evident in how the notion of Absolute Consciousness is defined and described. In the same Vedic text, we will find gender specific characteristics of the Absolute Being. The second stanza of the Aitreya Upanishad reads in the following manner:

"He created these worlds, viz. *ambhas, marici, mara* and *apah*. That which is beyond heaven is *ambhas*. Heaven is its support. The sky is *marici*. The earth is *mara*. The worlds that are below are the *apah*."

A shift occurs whereby, "It" becomes "He": and we all assume, and accept, that the Absolute Being has to be male. To follow this statement to its conclusion, we can state that as the Vedic texts equate the "Absolute Self" with the masculine, men are seen as being agents; in the second part of the <u>Aitreya Upanishad</u>, the first stanza reads: "In man indeed is the soul first conceived"; the implication is that men are agents in determining the birth of children while women are mere passive receptacles.

Biological sciences make use of these dichotomies, and feminists have critiqued how biology (which should be an objective science) makes use of the dominant trope of the "passive" female egg and the "active" male sperm. It is a notion that has also been used since times immemorial in the western worlds, beginning with Aristotle and St. Thomas.

There is no attempt by any religious institution to undress these entrenched misogyny that exists in Hinduism; and these dominant mainstream institutions simply reiterate the status quo. If we pick up a random text on religion that has been published by a well-recognized, religious institution, like the Ramakrishna Mission (that is seen as epitomising modern Hinduism), we find a similar trope operating as the subtext.

In <u>How is a man Reborn</u>, a short text that was published in 1970, by Advaita Ashrama, the publishing house of the Ramakrishna Mission, Swami Satprakashananda makes use of the same above mentioned dichotomy (pp.43-48); he cites instances from the <u>Chandogya Upanishad</u>, the <u>Brhadaranyaka Upanishad</u>, one Dr. Sturtevant, the <u>Aitareya Upanishad</u> and Sankara to prove the same point, whereby women are seen as passive agents whose only role in society is to procreate while men and sons do all the active work.

We can but make a beginning in dismantling these texts on Hinduism by re-transcribing them. The hope is that our daughters will be able to live in a gender —neutral society.

THE ARRANGEMENT OF THE TEXT:

ON THE LEFT SIDE, THERE IS THE OLDER VERSION OF THE **KATHA UPANISHAD AND THE RIGHT SIDE HAS A REVISED VERSION OF THE TEXT.**

PART I.
CANTO I.

Introduction: Salutation to Bhagavan Yama (Death), son of the Sun and the imparter of the knowledge of Brahman, and salutation to Naciket.

CANTO I.

Introduction: Salutation to Bhagavan Yama (Death), child of the Sun and the imparter of the knowledge of Brahman, and salutation to Naciket.

1. Once upon a time, the son of Vájasravá, being desirous of fruit, gave away everything. He has, as the story goes, a son named Naciket.

1. Once upon a time, the progeny of Vájaśravá, being desirous of fruit, gave away everything. S/he has, as the story goes, a child named Naciket/a.

2. As the presents were being carried (to the Bráhmanas) faith took possession of him who was still a boy. He thought:

2. As the presents were being carried (to the wise-religious invitees) faith took possession of the child who was still young. S/he thought:

3. He goes to those worlds that are known as joyless, who gives away the cows that have drunk water and eaten grass (for food), whose milk has been milked (for the last time), and which have lost their organs.

3.   S/he goes to those worlds that are known as joyless, who gives away the cows that have drunk water and eaten grass (for food), whose milk has been milked (for the last time), and which have lost their organs.

4. He said to his father,
    'Father, to whom will you
    offer me?' He spoke to him a
    second time and a third
    time. To him (the father)
    said, 'To Death I offer you.'

4.   S/he said to his guardian,
     'Parent, to whom will you
     offer me?' S/he spoke to him
     a second time and a third
     time. To the child, (the
     parent) said, 'To Death I
     offer you.'

5. Among many I rank as belonging to the highest; among many I rank as belonging to the middling. What purpose can there be of Death that my father will get achieved today through me?

5.   Among many I rank as belonging to the highest; among many I rank as belonging to the middling. What purpose can there be of Death that my parent will get achieved today through me?

6. Consider successively how your forefathers behaved, and consider how others behave (now). Man decays and dies like corn, and emerges again like corn.

6.   Consider successively how your fore-parents behaved, and consider how others behave (now). People decay and die like corn, and emerge again like corn.

7. A Bráhmana guest enters the houses like fire. For him they accomplish this kind of propitiation. O Death, carry water (for him).

7. A wise-religious guest enters the houses like fire. For that person they accomplish this kind of propitiation. O Death, carry water (for the guest).

8. If in anyone's house a Bráhmana guest abides without food, that Bráhmana destroys hope and expectation, the results of holy association and sweet discourse, sacrifices and charities, sons and cattle – all these – of that man of little intelligence.

8.   If in anyone's house a wise-religious guest abides without food, that wise-religious person destroys hope and expectation, the results of holy association and sweet discourse, sacrifices and charities, children and wealth – all these – of that person of little intelligence.

9. O Bráhmana, since you have
    lived in my house for three
    nights without food, a guest
    and an adorable person as
    you are, let my salutations
    be to you, and let good
    accrue to me (by averting
    the fault arising) from that
    (lapse). Ask for three boons
    – one in respect of each
    (night).

9. O wise-religious person, since you have lived in my house for three nights without food, a guest and an adorable person as you are, let my salutations be to you, and let good accrue to me (by averting the fault arising) from that (lapse). Ask for three boons – one in respect of each (night).

10. O Death, of the three boons I ask this one as the first, viz. that (my father) Gautama may become freed from anxiety, calm of mind, freed from anger towards me, and he may recognize me and talk to me when freed by you.

10. O Death, of the three boons I ask this one as the first, viz. that (my parent) Gautama/Gautami may become freed from anxiety, calm of mind, freed from anger towards me, and s/he may recognize me and talk to me when freed by you.

11. Having recognized (you), Auddálaki Ăruni will be (possessed of affection) just as he had before. Seeing you freed from the jaws of Death, he will get over his anger and will, with my permission, sleep happily for many a night.

11. Having recognized (you), your parent, the child of Aruna will be (possessed of affection) just as s/he had before. Seeing you freed from the jaws of Death, s/he will get over anger and will, with my permission, sleep happily for many a night.

12. In heaven there is no fear – you are not there, (and) nobody is struck with fear because of old age. Having transcended both hunger and thirst, and crossed over sorrow, one rejoices in the heavenly world.

12. In heaven there is no fear – you [Death] are not there, (and) nobody is struck with fear because of old age. Having transcended both hunger and thirst, and crossed over sorrow, one rejoices in the heavenly world.

13. O Death, such as you are, you know that Fire which leads to heaven. Of that you tell me who am full of faith. The dwellers of heaven get immortality. This I ask for through the second boon.

13. O Death, such as you are, you know that Fire which leads to heaven. Of that you tell me who am full of faith. The dwellers of heaven get immortality. This I ask for through the second boon.

14. **O Naciketá, being well aware of the Fire that is conducive to heaven, I shall tell you of it. That very thing you understand, with attention, from my words. That Fire which is the means for the attainment of heaven and which is the support of the world, know it to be established in the intellect (of the enlightened ones).**

14. O Naciketá, being well aware of the Fire that is conducive to heaven, I shall tell you of it. That very thing you understand, with attention, from my words. That Fire which is the means for the attainment of heaven and which is the support of the world, know it to be established in the intellect (of the enlightened ones).

15. Death told him of the Fire
that is the source of the
world, the class and number
of bricks, as also the manner
of arranging for the fire. And
he (Naciketá), too, repeated
verbatim, with
understanding, all these as
they were spoken. Then
Death, being satisfied with
this, said again:

15. Death told Naciketá of the Fire that is the source of the world, the class and number of bricks, as also the manner of arranging for the fire. And s/he (Naciketá), too, repeated verbatim, with understanding, all these as they were spoken. Then Death, being satisfied with this, said again:

16. Feeling delighted, that high-souled one said to him, 'Out of favour towards you, I now grant again another boon. This fire will be known by your name indeed. And accept this multiformed necklace as well.

16. Feeling delighted, that high-souled one [Death] said to Naciketá, 'Out of favour towards you, I now grant again another boon. This fire will be known by your name indeed. And accept this multiformed necklace as well.

17. 'One who, getting connection with the three, piles up the Naciketá fire thrice, and undertakes three kinds of work, crosses over death. Getting knowledge of that omniscient One who is born of Brahmá and is the praiseworthy Deity, and realizing Him, he attains this peace fully.

17. 'One who, getting connection with the three, piles up the Naciketá fire thrice, and undertakes three kinds of work, crosses over death. Getting knowledge of that omniscient One who is born of Brahmá and is the praiseworthy Deity, and realizing Her/ Him, s/he attains this peace fully.

18. 'One who performs the Náciketa sacrifice thrice after having known these three (factors), and he who having known thus, accomplishes the Náciketa sacrifice, casts off the snares of Death even earlier, and crossing over sorrow rejoices in heaven.

18. 'One who performs the Náciketa sacrifice thrice after having known these three (factors), and s/he who having known thus, accomplishes the Náciketa sacrifice, casts off the snares of Death even earlier, and crossing over sorrow rejoices in heaven.

19. 'O Naciketá, this is for you the boon about the Fire that leads to heaven, for which you prayed through the second boon. People will speak of this Fire as yours indeed. O Naciketá, ask for the third boon.'

44

19. 'O Naciketá, this is for you the boon about the Fire that leads to heaven, for which you prayed through the second boon. People will speak of this Fire as yours indeed. O Naciketá, ask for the third boon.'

20. This doubt that arises, consequent on the death of a man – some saying, 'It exists', and others saying 'It does not exist' – I would know this, under your instruction. Of all the boons, this one is the third boon.

20. This doubt that arises, consequent on the death of a person – some saying, 'It exists', and others saying 'It does not exist' – I would know this, under your instruction. Of all the boons, this one is the third boon.

21. With regard to this, even the gods entertained doubts in days of yore; for being subtle, this substance (the Self) is not truly comprehended. O Naciketá, ask for some other boon; do not press me; give up this (boon) that is demanded of me.

21. With regard to this, even the Divine Beings entertained doubts in days of yore; for being subtle, this substance (the Self) is not truly comprehended. O Naciketá, ask for some other boon; do not press me; give up this (boon) that is demanded of me.

22. Even the gods entertained doubt with regard to this thing; and O Death, since you too say that It is not truly comprehended and since any other instructor like you, of this think, is not to be had, (therefore) there is no other boon comparable to this one.

22. Even the gods entertained doubt with regard to this thing; and O Death, since you too say that It is not truly comprehended and since any other instructor like you, of this think, is not to be had, (therefore) there is no other boon comparable to this one.

23. Ask for sons and grandsons that will be centenarians. Ask for many animals, elephants, and gold, and horses, and a vast expanse of the earth. And you yourself live for as many years as you like.

23. Ask for children and grandchildren that will be centenarians. Ask for many animals, elephants, and gold, and horses, and a vast expanse of the earth. And you yourself live for as many years as you like.

24. If you think some other boon to be equal to this, ask for that. Ask for wealth and long life. O Naciketá, you become (a ruler) over a vast region. I make you fit for the enjoyment of (all) delectable things.

24. If you think some other boon to be equal to this, ask for that. Ask for wealth and long life. O Naciketá, you become (a ruler) over a vast region. I make you fit for the enjoyment of (all) delectable things.

25. Whatever things there be that are desirable but difficult to get – pray for all those cherished things according to your choice. Here are these women with chariots and musical instruments – such are surely not to be had by mortals. With these, who are offered by me, you get yourself served. O Naciketá, do not inquire about death.

25. Whatever things there be that are desirable but difficult to get – pray for all those cherished things according to your choice. Here are these women and men with chariots and musical instruments – such are surely not to be had by mortals. With these, who are offered by me, you get yourself served. O Naciketá, do not inquire about death.

26. O Death, ephemeral are these, and they waste away the vigour of all the organs that a man has. All life, without exception, is short indeed. Let the vehicles be yours alone; let the dances and songs be yours.

26. O Death, ephemeral are these, and they waste away the vigour of all the organs that a person has. All life, without exception, is short indeed. Let the vehicles be yours alone; let the dances and songs be yours.

27. Man is not to be satisfied with wealth. Now that we have met you, we shall get wealth. We shall live as long as you will rule. But the boon that is worth praying for by me is that alone.

27. A person is not to be satisfied with wealth. Now that we have met you, we shall get wealth. We shall live as long as you will rule. But the boon that is worth praying for by me is that alone.

28. Having reached the proximity of the undecaying immortals, what decaying mortal who dwells on this lower region, the earth, but knows of higher goals, will take delight in a long life while conscious of the worthlessness of music, disport, and the joy thereof.

28. Having reached the proximity of the undecaying immortals, what decaying mortal who dwells on this lower region, the earth, but knows of higher goals, will take delight in a long life while conscious of the worthlessness of music, disport, and the joy thereof?

29. **O Death, tell us of that thing about which people entertain doubt in the context of the next world and whose knowledge leads to a great result. Apart from this boon, which relates to the inscrutable thing, Naciketá does not pray for any other.**

29. **O Death, tell us of that thing about which people entertain doubt in the context of the next world and whose knowledge leads to a great result. Apart from this boon, which relates to the inscrutable thing, Naciketá does not pray for any other.**

PART I.
CANTO II.

1. The preferable is different
    indeed; and so, indeed, is the
    pleasurable different. These
    two, serving divergent
    purposes, (as they do), bind
    men. Good befalls him who
    accepts the preferable among
    these two. He who selects
    the pleasurable, falls from
    the true end.

1. The preferable is different indeed; and so, indeed, is the pleasurable different. These two, serving divergent purposes, (as they do), bind people. Good befalls the person who accepts the preferable among these two. S/he who selects the pleasurable, falls from the true end.

2. The preferable and the pleasurable approach man. The man of intelligence, having considered them, separates the two. The intelligent one selects the electable in preference to the delectable; the non-intelligent one selects the delectable for the sake of growth and protection (of the body etc.).

2. The preferable and the pleasurable approach a person. The person of intelligence, having considered them, separates the two. The intelligent one selects the electable in preference to the delectable; the non-intelligent one selects the delectable for the sake of growth and protection (of the body etc.).

3. O Naciketá! you, such as you are, have discarded, after consideration, all the desirable things that are themselves delightful or are the producers of delight. You have not accepted this path of wealth in which many a man comes to grief.

3. O Naciketá! you, such as you
    are, have discarded, after
    consideration, all the
    desirable things that are
    themselves delightful or are
    the producers of delight.
    You have not accepted this
    path of wealth in which
    many a person comes to
    grief.

4. That which is known as knowledge and that which is known as ignorance are widely contradictory, and they follow divergent courses. I consider Naciketá to be an aspirant for knowledge, (because) the enjoyable things, multifarious though they be, did not tempt you.

4. That which is known as knowledge and that which is known as ignorance are widely contradictory, and they follow divergent courses. I consider Naciketá to be an aspirant for knowledge, (because) the enjoyable things, multifarious though they be, did not tempt you.

5. Living in the midst of ignorance and considering themselves intelligent and enlightened, the senseless people go round and round, following crooked courses, just like the blind led by the blind.

5. Living in the midst of ignorance and considering themselves intelligent and enlightened, the senseless people go round and round, following crooked courses, just like the blind led by the blind.

6. The means for the attainment of the other world does not become revealed to the non-discriminating man who blunders, being befooled by the lure of wealth. One that constantly thinks that there is only this world, and none hereafter, comes under my sway again and again.

6. The means for the attainment of the other world does not become revealed to the non-discriminating person who blunders, being befooled by the lure of wealth. One that constantly thinks that there is only this world, and none hereafter, comes under my sway again and again.

7. Of that (Self), which is not available for the mere hearing to many, (and) which many do not understand even while hearing, the expounder is wonderful and the receiver is wonderful; wonderful is he who knows under the instruction of an adept.

7.   Of that (Self), which is not available for the mere hearing to many, (and) which many do not understand even while hearing, the expounder is wonderful and the receiver is wonderful; wonderful is the person who knows under the instruction of an adept.

8. The Self is not certainly adequately known when spoken of by an inferior person; for It is thought of variously. When taught by one who has become identified with It, there is no further cogitation with regard to It. For It is beyond argumentation, being subtler even than the atomic structure.

8. The Self is not certainly adequately known when spoken of by an inferior person; for It is thought of variously. When taught by one who has become identified with It, there is no further cogitation with regard to It. For It is beyond argumentation, being subtler even than the atomic structure.

9. This wisdom that you have, O dearest one, which leads to sound knowledge when imparted only by someone else (other than the logician), is not to be attained through argumentation. You are, O compassionable one, endowed with true resolution. May our questioner be like you, O Naciketá.

9. This wisdom that you have, O dearest one, which leads to sound knowledge when imparted only by someone else (other than the logician), is not to be attained through argumentation. You are, O compassionable one, endowed with true resolution. May our questioner be like you, O Naciketá.

10. (Since) I know that this treasure is impermanent — for that permanent entity cannot be attained through impermanent things — therefore (knowingly) did I pile up the Naciketá fire with impermanent things, and have (thereby) attained (relative) permanence.

10. (Since) I know that this treasure is impermanent – for that permanent entity cannot be attained through impermanent things – therefore (knowingly) did I pile up the Naciketá fire with impermanent things, and have (thereby) attained (relative) permanence.

11. **O Naciketá, you, on becoming enlightened, have rejected (them all) by examining patiently the highest reach of desire, the support of the universe, the infinite results of meditation, the other shore of fearlessness, the extensive course of (Hiranyagarbha) that is praiseworthy and great, as also (your own) state.**

11. O Naciketá, you, on becoming enlightened, have rejected (them all) by examining patiently the highest reach of desire, the support of the universe, the infinite results of meditation, the other shore of fearlessness, the extensive course of (Hiranyagarbha) that is praiseworthy and great, as also (your own) state.

12. The intelligent man gives up happiness and sorrow by developing concentration of mind on the Self and thereby meditating on the old Deity who is inscrutable, lodged inaccessibly, located in the intellect, and seated in the midst of misery.

12. The intelligent person gives up happiness and sorrow by developing concentration of mind on the Self and thereby meditating on the old Deity who is inscrutable, lodged inaccessibly, located in the intellect, and seated in the midst of misery.

13. After hearing this, grasping it fully, separating this righteous thing (from the body etc.), and attaining this subtle thing, that mortal rejoices, for he has obtained that which is the cause of delight. I consider that the mansion (of Brahma) is wide, open to Naciketá.

13. After hearing this, grasping it fully, separating this righteous thing (from the body etc.), and attaining this subtle thing, that mortal rejoices, for s/he has obtained that which is the cause of delight. I consider that the mansion (of Brahma) is wide, open to Naciketá.

14. 'Tell (me) of that thing which you see as different from virtue, different from vice, different from this cause and effect, and different from the past and the future.'

14. 'Tell (me) of that thing which you see as different from virtue, different from vice, different from this cause and effect, and different from the past and the future.'

15. I tell you briefly of that goal which all the Vedas with one voice propound, which all the austerities speak of, and wishing for which people practice Brahmacarya: it is this, viz *Om.*

15. I tell you briefly of that goal which all the Vedas with one voice propound, which all the austerities speak of, and wishing for which people practice meditative contemplation: it is this, viz *Om.*

16. This letter (*Om*), indeed, is the (inferior) Brahman (Hiranyagarbha); and this letter is, indeed, the supreme Brahman. Anybody, who, (while) meditating on this letter, wants any of the two, to him comes that.

16. This letter (*Om*), indeed, is the (inferior) Brahman (Hiranyagarbha); and this letter is, indeed, the supreme Brahman. Anybody, who, (while) meditating on this letter, wants any of the two, to her/him comes that.

17. This medium is the best; this medium is the supreme (and the inferior) Brahman. Meditating on this medium, one becomes adorable in the world of Brahman.

17. This medium is the best; this medium is the supreme (and the inferior) Brahman. Meditating on this medium, one becomes adorable in the world of Brahman.

18. The intelligent Self is neither born nor does It die. It did not originate from anything, nor did anything originate from It. It is birthless, eternal, undecaying, and ancient. It is not injured even when the body is killed.

18. The intelligent Self is neither born nor does It die. It did not originate from anything, nor did anything originate from It. It is birthless, eternal, undecaying, and ancient. It is not injured even when the body is killed.

19. If the killer thinks (of It) in terms of killing and if the killed thinks (of It) as killed, both of them do not know. It does not kill, nor is It killed.

19. If the killer thinks (of It) in terms of killing and if the killed thinks (of It) as killed, both of them do not know. It does not kill, nor is It killed.

20. The Self that is subtler than the subtle and greater than the great, is lodged in the heart of (every) creature. A desireless man sees that glory of the Self through the serenity of the organs, and (thereby he becomes) free from sorrow.

20. The Self that is subtler than the subtle and greater than the great, is lodged in the heart of (every) creature. A desireless person sees that glory of the Self through the serenity of the organs, and (thereby s/he becomes) free from sorrow.

21. While sitting, It travels far away; while sleeping, It goes everywhere. Who but I can know that Deity who is both joyful and joyless?

21. While sitting, It travels far away; while sleeping, It goes everywhere. Who but I can know that Deity who is both joyful and joyless?

22. Having meditated on the Self, as bodiless in the midst of bodies, as permanent in the midst of the impermanent, and as great and pervasive, the wise man does not grieve.

22. Having meditated on the Self, as bodiless in the midst of bodies, as permanent in the midst of the impermanent, and as great and pervasive, the wise person does not grieve.

23. This Self cannot be known through much study, nor through the intellect, nor through much hearing. It can be known through the Self alone that the aspirant prays to; this Self of that seeker reveals Its true nature.

23. This Self cannot be known through much study, nor through the intellect, nor through much hearing. It can be known through the Self alone that the aspirant prays to; this Self of that seeker reveals Its true nature.

24. One who has not desisted from bad conduct, whose senses are not under control, whose mind is not concentrated, whose mind is not free from anxiety (about the result of concentration), cannot attain this Self through knowledge.

24. One who has not desisted from bad conduct, whose senses are not under control, whose mind is not concentrated, whose mind is not free from anxiety (about the result of concentration), cannot attain this Self through knowledge.

25. How can one know thus as to
where It (the Self) is, for
which both the Bráhmana
and the Ksatriya become
food, and for which death
takes the place of a curry?

25. How can one know thus as to where It (the Self) is, for which both the wise-religious one and the brave warrior become food, and for which death takes the place of a curry?

PART I.
Canto III.

1. The knowers of Brahman, the worshippers of the five fires, and those who perform the Naciketá sacrifice thrice, compare to shade and light, the two enjoyers of the inevitable results of work, who have entered within the body, into the cavity (of the heart) which is the supreme abode of the Most High (Brahman).

1. The knowers of Brahman, the worshippers of the five fires, and those who perform the Naciketá sacrifice thrice, compare to shade and light, the two enjoyers of the inevitable results of work, who have entered within the body, into the cavity (of the heart) which is the supreme abode of the Most High (Brahman).

2. We have known that Náciketa Fire, which is the bridge for the sacrificers, as also that which is the undecaying supreme Brahman beyond fear for those who want to cross over (the world).

2. We have known that Náciketa Fire, which is the bridge for the sacrificers, as also that which is the undecaying supreme Brahman beyond fear for those who want to cross over (the world).

3. Know the (individual) self as the master of the chariot, and the body as the chariot. Know the intellect as the charioteer, and the mind as verily the bridle.

3. Know the (individual) self as the controller of the chariot, and the body as the chariot. Know the intellect as the charioteer, and the mind as verily the bridle.

4. They call the organs the horses; the organs having been imagined as horses, (know) the objects as the roads. The discriminating people call that Self the enjoyer when It is associated with body-organs, and mind.

4. They call the organs the horses; the organs having been imagined as horses, (know) the objects as the roads. The discriminating people call that Self the enjoyer when It is associated with body-organs, and mind.

5. But the organs of that intellect, which, being ever associated with an uncontrolled mind, becomes devoid of discrimination, are unruly like the vicious horses of the charioteer.

5. But the organs of that intellect, which, being ever associated with an uncontrolled mind, becomes devoid of discrimination, are unruly like the vicious horses of the charioteer.

6. But of that (intellect) which, being ever associated with a restrained mind, is endowed with discrimination, the organs are controllable like the good horses of the charioteer.

6. But of that (intellect) which, being ever associated with a restrained mind, is endowed with discrimination, the organs are controllable like the good horses of the charioteer.

7. But he, (that master of the chariot), does not attain that goal (through that intellect), who, being associated with a non-discriminating intellect and an uncontrollable mind, is ever impure; and he attains worldly existence.

7. But s/he, (that controller of the chariot), does not attain that goal (through that intellect), who, being associated with a non-discriminating intellect and an uncontrollable mind, is ever impure; and s/he attains worldly existence.

8. That (master of the chariot), however, who is associated with a discriminating intellect, and being endowed with a controlled mind, is ever pure, attains that goal from which he is not born again.

8. That (controller of the chariot), however, who is associated with a discriminating intellect, and being endowed with a controlled mind, is ever pure, attains that goal from which s/he is not born again.

9. The man, however, who has as his charioteer a discriminating intellect, and who has under control the reins of the mind, attains the end of the road; and that is the highest place of Visnu.

9. The person, however, who has as its charioteer a discriminating intellect, and who has under control the reins of the mind, attains the end of the road; and that is the highest place of the Supreme Being.

10. The sense-objects are higher than the senses, and the mind is higher than the sense-objects; but the intellect is higher than the mind, and the Great Soul is higher than the intellect.

10. The sense-objects are higher than the senses, and the mind is higher than the sense-objects; but the intellect is higher than the mind, and the Great Soul is higher than the intellect.

11. The Unmanifested is higher than Mahat; the Purusa is higher than the Unmanifested. There is nothing higher than the Purusa. He is the culmination. He is the highest goal.

11. The Unmanifested is higher than Mahat; the Purusa is higher than the Unmanifested. There is nothing higher than the Purusa. S/he is the culmination. S/he is the highest goal.

12. He is hidden in all beings, and hence He does not appear as the Self (of all). But by the seers of subtle things, He is seen through a pointed and fine intellect.

12. S/he is hidden in all beings, and hence S/he does not appear as the Self (of all). But by the seers of subtle things, S/he is seen through a pointed and fine intellect.

13. The discriminating man should merge the (organ of) speech into the mind; he should merge that (mind) into the intelligent self; he should merge the intelligent self into the Great Soul; he should merge the Great Soul into the peaceful Self.

13. The discriminating person should merge the (organ of) speech into the mind; s/he should merge that (mind) into the intelligent self; s/he should merge the intelligent self into the Great Soul; s/he should merge the Great Soul into the peaceful Self.

14. Arise, awake, and learn by approaching the excellent ones. The wise ones describe that path to be as impassable as a razor's edge, which, when sharpened, is difficult to tread on.

14. Arise, awake, and learn by approaching the excellent ones. The wise ones describe that path to be as impassable as a razor's edge, which, when sharpened, is difficult to tread on.

15. One becomes freed from the jaws of death by knowing That which is soundless, touchless, colourless, undiminishing, and also tasteless, eternal, odourless, without beginning, and without end, distinct from Mahat, and ever constant.

15. One becomes freed from the jaws of death by knowing That which is soundless, touchless, colourless, undiminishing, and also tasteless, eternal, odourless, without beginning, and without end, distinct from Mahat, and ever constant.

16. Relating and hearing this eternal anecdote – as received by Naciketá and as told by Death – the intelligent man becomes glorified in the region that is Brahman.

16. **Relating and hearing this eternal anecdote – as received by Naciketá and as told by Death – the intelligent person becomes glorified in the region that is Brahman.**

17. Should anyone, after purification, get this highest secret recited before an assembly of Bráhmanas, or at the time of the ceremonies for the dead, (then) that (ceremony) becomes conducive to eternal result.

17. Should anyone, after purification, get this highest secret recited before an assembly of wise-religious people, or at the time of the ceremonies for the dead, (then) that (ceremony) becomes conducive to eternal result.

PART II.
Canto I.

1. The self-existent Lord destroyed the outgoing senses. Therefore, one sees the outer things and not the inner Self. A rare discriminating man, desiring immortality, turns his eyes away and then sees the indwelling Self.

1. The self-existent Supreme
    Being destroyed the
    outgoing senses. Therefore,
    one sees the outer things and
    not the inner Self. A rare
    discriminating person,
    desiring immortality, turns
    its eyes away and then sees
    the indwelling Self.

2. The unintelligent people follow the external desires. They get entangled in the snares of the wide-spread death. Therefore, the discriminating people, having known what true immortality is in the midst of impermanent things, do not pray for anything here.

2. The unintelligent people
   follow the external desires.
   They get entangled in the
   snares of the wide-spread
   death. Therefore, the
   discriminating people,
   having known what true
   immortality is in the midst of
   impermanent things, do not
   pray for anything here.

3. What remains here
    (unknowable to this Self)
    through which very Self
    people perceive colour, taste,
    smell, sound, touch, and
    sexual pleasure? This indeed
    is that (Self asked for by
    Naciketá).

3. What remains here (unknowable to this Self) through which very Self people perceive colour, taste, smell, sound, touch, and sexual pleasure? This indeed is that (Self asked for by Naciketá).

4. Having realized the great and all-pervading Self, through which a man perceives the objects in both the sleep and the waking states, a wise man does not grieve.

4. Having realized the great and all-pervading Self, through which a person perceives the objects in both the sleep and the waking states, a wise person does not grieve.

5.   Anyone who knows proximately this Self – the enjoyer of the fruits of works, the supporter of life etc. – as the lord of the past and the future, does not want to save (the Self) just because of that (knowledge). This indeed is that.

5. Anyone who knows proximately this Self – the enjoyer of the fruits of works, the supporter of life etc. – as the controller of the past and the future, does not want to save (the Self) just because of that (knowledge). This indeed is that.

6. He sees this very aforesaid Brahman who sees the First Born (Hiranyagarbha) – born before the five elements from Consciousness (Brahman) – as existing in the cavity of the heart in the midst of body and senses, after having entered there.

6. S/he sees this very aforesaid Brahman who sees the First Born (Hiranyagarbha) – born before the five elements from Consciousness (Brahman) – as existing in the cavity of the heart in the midst of body and senses, after having entered there.

7. He (sees) that very Brahman (who sees) that Aditi, comprising all the deities, who takes birth as Hiranyagarbha, who is manifested in association with the elements, and who is seated in the cavity of the heart, after entering there.

7. S/he (sees) that very Brahman (who sees) that Aditi, comprising all the deities, who takes birth as Hiranyagarbha, who is manifested in association with the elements, and who is seated in the cavity of the heart, after entering there.

8. The sacrificial Fire lodged in two fire-producing pieces of wood, (as also the Fire lodged in the hearts of Yogis) that is well protected – just as much as the foetus by pregnant women – and the Fire that is adorable every day by vigilant men with oblation (and contemplation) – that Fire too is but this Brahman.

8. The sacrificial Fire lodged in
two fire-producing pieces of
wood, (as also the Fire
lodged in the hearts of
Yogi/nis) that is well
protected – just as much as
the foetus by pregnant
women – and the Fire that is
adorable every day by
vigilant people with oblation
(and contemplation) – that
Fire too is but this Brahman.

9. On that, from which the sun rises and in which it sets, are fixed all the deities. None ever transcends that. This indeed is that.

9. On that, from which the sun rises and in which it sets, are fixed all the deities. None ever transcends that. This indeed is that.

10. What indeed is here, is there; what is there, is here likewise. He who sees as though there is difference here, goes from death to death.

10. What indeed is here, is there; what is there, is here likewise. S/he who sees as though there is difference here, goes from death to death.

11. This is to be attained through the mind indeed. There is no diversity here whatsoever. He who sees as though there is difference here, goes from death to death.

11. This is to be attained through the mind indeed. There is no diversity here whatsoever. S/he who sees as though there is difference here, goes from death to death.

12. The Being (Purusa), of the
size of a thumb, resides in
the body. Knowing Him as
the ruler of the past and the
future, one does not want, by
virtue of that knowledge, to
save the Self. This indeed is
that.

12. The Being (Purusa), of the size of a thumb, resides in the body. Knowing It as the ruler of the past and the future, one does not want, by virtue of that knowledge, to save the Self. This indeed is that.

13. The Purusa, who is of the size of a thumb, is like a light without smoke. He is the ruler of the past and the future. He exists today, and He will exist tomorrow. This indeed is that.

13. The Purusa, who is of the size of a thumb, is like a light without smoke. S/he is the ruler of the past and the future. S/he exists today, and S/he will exist tomorrow. This indeed is that.

14. As water rained on an inaccessible height gets dispersed on (lower) hilly regions, similarly, one who perceives the selves differently, runs after them only.

14. As water rained on an inaccessible height gets dispersed on (lower) hilly regions, similarly, one who perceives the selves differently, runs after them only.

15. O Gautama, as pure water poured on pure water becomes verily the same, so also does become the Self of the man of knowledge who is given to deliberation (on the Self).

15. O Gautami/a, as pure water poured on pure water becomes verily the same, so also does become the Self of the person of knowledge who is given to deliberation (on the Self).

PART II.
Canto II.

1. Of the unborn One, whose consciousness is unflickering, there is a city with eleven gates. Meditating (on Him), one does not grieve and, becoming freed, one becomes emancipated. This indeed is that.

1. Of the unborn One, whose consciousness is unflickering, there is a city with eleven gates. Meditating (on It), one does not grieve and, becoming freed, one becomes emancipated. This indeed is that.

2. As the moving (sun) He dwells in heaven; (as air) He pervades all and dwells in the inter-space; as fire He resides on the earth; as Soma He stays in a jar; He lives among men; He lives among gods; He dwells in truth; He dwells in space; He is born in water; He takes birth from the earth; He is born in the sacrifice; He emerges from the mountains; He is unchanging; and He is great.

2. As the moving (sun) S/he dwells in heaven; (as air) S/he pervades all and dwells in the inter-space; as fire S/he resides on the earth; as Soma S/he stays in a jar; S/he lives among men; S/he lives among gods; S/he dwells in truth; S/he dwells in space; S/he is born in water; S/he takes birth from the earth; S/he is born in the sacrifice; S/he emerges from the mountains; S/he is unchanging; and S/he is great.

3. All deities worship that adorable One sitting in the middle, who pushes the *prána* upward and impels the *apána* inward.

3. All deities worship that adorable One sitting in the middle, who pushes the *prána* upward and impels the *apána* inward.

4. When this dweller in the body becomes detached, when He is freed from this body, what else remains here (in this body)? This indeed is that.

4. When this dweller in the body becomes detached, when S/he is freed from this body, what else remains here (in this body)? This indeed is that.

5. No mortal lives by *prána* or *apana*; but all live by something else due to which these two find asylum.

5. No mortal lives by *prána* or *apana*; but all live by something else due to which these two find asylum.

6. Well, O Gautama, I shall tell you of this secret, eternal Brahman; and also how the Self fares after death.

6. Well, O Gautami/a, I shall tell you of this secret, eternal Brahman; and also how the Self fares after death.

7. Some souls enter the womb
   for acquiring bodies and
   others follow the motionless,
   in accordance with their
   work and in conformity with
   their knowledge.

7. Some souls enter the womb
    for acquiring bodies and
    others follow the motionless,
    in accordance with their
    work and in conformity with
    their knowledge.

8. That Purusa indeed, who keeps awake and goes on creating desirable things even when the senses fall asleep, is pure; and He is Brahman, and He is called the Immortal. All the worlds are fixed on Him; none can transcend Him. This indeed is that.

8. That Purusa indeed, who keeps awake and goes on creating desirable things even when the senses fall asleep, is pure; and S/he is Brahman, and S/he is called the Immortal. All the worlds are fixed on It; none can transcend It. This indeed is that.

9. Just as fire, though one, having entered the world, assumes separate forms in respect of different shapes, similarly, the Self inside all beings, though one, assumes a form in respect of each shape; and (yet) It is outside.

9. Just as fire, though one, having entered the world, assumes separate forms in respect of different shapes, similarly, the Self inside all beings, though one, assumes a form in respect of each shape; and (yet) It is outside.

10. As air, though one, having entered into this world, assumes separate forms in respect of different shapes, similarly, the Self inside all beings, though one, assumes a form in respect of each shape; and (yet) It is outside.

10. As air, though one, having entered into this world, assumes separate forms in respect of different shapes, similarly, the Self inside all beings, though one, assumes a form in respect of each shape; and (yet) It is outside.

11. Just as the sun, which is the eye of the whole world, is not tainted by the ocular and external defects, similarly, the Self, that is but one in all beings, is not tainted by the sorrows of the world, It being transcendental.

11. Just as the sun, which is the eye of the whole world, is not tainted by the ocular and external defects, similarly, the Self, that is but one in all beings, is not tainted by the sorrows of the world, It being transcendental.

12. Eternal peace is for those – and not for others – who are discriminating and who realize in their hearts Him who – being one, the controller, and the inner Self of all - makes a single form multifarious.

12. Eternal peace is for those –
    and not for others – who are
    discriminating and who
    realize in their hearts It/
    Her/Him who – being one,
    the controller, and the inner
    Self of all - makes a single
    form multifarious.

13. Eternal peace is for those – and not for others – who are discriminating and who realize in their hearts Him who – being the eternal among the ephemeral, the consciousness among the conscious – alone dispenses the desired objects to many.

13. Eternal peace is for those –
and not for others – who are
discriminating and who
realize in their hearts It/
Her/ Him who – being the
eternal among the
ephemeral, the
consciousness among the
conscious – alone dispenses
the desired objects to many.

14. How shall I know that supreme, unspeakable Bliss which they realize directly as 'This'? Is It self-effulgent – does It shine distinctly, or does It not?

14. How shall I know that supreme, unspeakable Bliss which they realize directly as 'This'? Is It self-effulgent – does It shine distinctly, or does It not?

15. There the sun does not shine, neither do the moon and the stars; nor do these flashes of lightning shine. How can this fire? He shining, all these shine; through his lustre all these are variously illumined.

15. There the sun does not shine, neither do the moon and the stars; nor do these flashes of lightning shine. How can this fire? S/he shining, all these shine; through its lustre all these are variously illumined.

PART II.
Canto III.

1. This is the beginningless peepul tree that has its roots above and branches down. That (which is its root) is pure, that is Brahman and that is called immortal. On that are fixed all the worlds; none transcends that. This verily is that.

1. This is the beginningless peepul tree that has its roots above and branches down. That (which is its root) is pure, that is Brahman and that is called immortal. On that are fixed all the worlds; none transcends that. This verily is that.

2. All this universe that there is, emerges and moves because there is the supreme Brahman which is a great terror like an uplifted thunderbolt. Those who know this become immortal.

2. All this universe that there is, emerges and moves because there is the supreme Brahman which is a great terror like an uplifted thunderbolt. Those who know this become immortal.

3. From fear of Him fire burns,
    from fear shines the Sun;
    from fear run Indra and Air,
    and Death the fifth.

3.   From fear of Her/ Him/ It
fire burns, from fear shines
the Sun; from fear run Indra
and Air, and Death the fifth.

4. If one succeeds in realizing
    here before the falling of the
    body, (one becomes freed);
    (else) because of that
    (failure) one becomes fit for
    embodiment in the worlds of
    creatures.

4. If one succeeds in realizing here before the falling of the body, (one becomes freed); (else) because of that (failure) one becomes fit for embodiment in the worlds of creatures.

5. As (one sees) in a mirror, so in one's intellect; as in a dream, so in the world of the manes, as it is seen in water, so in the world of the Gandharvas. As it is in the case of shade and light, so in the world of Brahma.

5. As (one sees) in a mirror, so in one's intellect; as in a dream, so in the world of the manes, as it is seen in water, so in the world of the Gandharvas. As it is in the case of shade and light, so in the world of Brahma.

6. Having known the dissimilarity of the senses that originate separately, as also their rising and setting, the intelligent man does not grieve.

6. Having known the dissimilarity of the senses that originate separately, as also their rising and setting, the intelligent person does not grieve.

7. The mind is superior to the organs; the intellect is superior to the mind; Mahat (the Great Soul) is superior to the intellect; the Unmanifested is superior to Mahat.

7. The mind is superior to the organs; the intellect is superior to the mind; Mahat (the Great Soul) is superior to the intellect; the Unmanifested is superior to Mahat.

8. But superior to the Unmanifested is the Purusa who is pervasive and is, indeed, without worldly attributes, knowing whom a man becomes freed and attains immortality.

8.   But superior to the Unmanifested is the Purusa who is pervasive and is, indeed, without worldly attributes, knowing whom a person becomes freed and attains immortality.

9. His form does not exist within the range of vision; nobody sees Him with the eye. When this Self is revealed through deliberation, It is realized by the intellect, the ruler of the mind, that resides in the heart. Those who know this become immortal.

9. Its form does not exist within the range of vision; nobody sees It with the eye. When this Self is revealed through deliberation, It is realized by the intellect, the ruler of the mind, that resides in the heart. Those who know this become immortal.

10. When the five senses of knowledge come to rest together with the mind, and the intellect, too, does not function, that state they call the highest.

10. When the five senses of knowledge come to rest together with the mind, and the intellect, too, does not function, that state they call the highest.

11. They consider that keeping of the senses steady as yoga. One becomes vigilant at that time, for yoga is subject to growth and decay.

11. They consider that keeping of the senses steady as yoga. One becomes vigilant at that time, for yoga is subject to growth and decay.

12. It cannot be attained through speech, nor through mind, nor through eye. How can It be known to anyone apart from him who speaks of It as existing?

12. It cannot be attained through speech, nor through mind, nor through eye. How can It be known to anyone apart from the person who speaks of It as existing?

13. The Self is (first) to be realized as existing, and (then) as It really is. Of these two (aspects), the real nature of the Self that has been known as merely existing, becomes favourably disposed (for self revelation).

13. The Self is (first) to be realized as existing, and (then) as It really is. Of these two (aspects),the real nature of the Self that has been known as merely existing, becomes favourably disposed (for self revelation).

14. When all desires clinging to one's heart fall off, then a mortal becomes immortal (and he) attains Brahman here.

14. When all desires clinging to one's heart fall off, then a mortal becomes immortal (and s/he) attains Brahman here.

15. When all the knots of the heart are destroyed, even while a man is alive, then a mortal becomes immortal. This much alone is the instruction (of all the Upanishads).

15. When all the knots of the heart are destroyed, even while a person is alive, then a mortal becomes immortal. This much alone is the instruction (of all the Upanishads).

16. The nerves of the heart are a hundred and one in number. Of them one passes through (the crown of) the head. Going up through that (nerve) one gets immortality. The others that have different directions, become the causes of death.

16. The nerves of the heart are a hundred and one in number. Of them one passes through (the crown of) the head. Going up through that (nerve) one gets immortality. The others that have different directions, become the causes of death.

17. The Purusa, the indwelling Self, of the size of a thumb, is ever seated in the hearts of men. One should unerringly separate Him from one's body like a stalk from the Múnja grass. Him one should know as pure and immortal. Him one should know as pure and immortal.

17. The Purusa, the indwelling Self, of the size of a thumb, is ever seated in the hearts of people. One should unerringly separate It from one's body like a stalk from the Múnja grass. It one should know as pure and immortal. It one should know as pure and immortal.

18. Naciketá, having first become free from virtue and vice, as also desire and ignorance, by acquiring this knowledge imparted by Death, as also the process of yoga in its totality, attained Brahman. Anyone else, too, who becomes a knower thus (like Naciketá) of the indwelling Self, (attains Brahman).

18. Naciketá, having first become free from virtue and vice, as also desire and ignorance, by acquiring this knowledge imparted by Death, as also the process of yoga in its totality, attained Brahman. Anyone else, too, who becomes a knower thus (like Naciketá) of the indwelling Self, (attains Brahman).

19. May He protect us both (by revealing knowledge). May He protect us both (by vouchsafing the results of knowledge). May we attain vigour together. Let what we study be invigorating. May we not cavil at each other. *Om*! Peace! Peace! Peace!

19. May S/he protect us both (by revealing knowledge). May S/he protect us both (by vouchsafing the results of knowledge). May we attain vigour together. Let what we study be invigorating. May we not cavil at each other. *Om*! Peace! Peace! Peace!

ABOUT THE AUTHOR

I grew up in an uber-brahmanical family where ritualistic worship was a part of my everyday life; the Vedic texts and the Upanishads were also something I grew up. I always thought that religion was something "out" there; I never actually thought that we were meant to believe in these texts on "revealed knowledge" in an absolute manner. But religion pervades every and all aspects of our lives – institutional, private or public, and be they secular, or not.

After reading the Hindu religious texts for myself, I realised how gendered these texts were, and to our sensibilities, the archaic notions that underlie the basic tenets of Hinduism sound ridiculous and perverse. We forget that the "revealed knowledge" that is evident in the Upanishads has been written by men, and their gender predetermined how they translated the notions of the Absolute Being into language.

 I do not want my daughter to grow up within such a flawed belief system; we have to dismantle the existing religious texts as they are and re-transcribe them in order to arrive at gender-neutral concepts of religion, and Being.